Understand Women Better

Lorin Krenn

Please read this

The author makes no guarantees concerning the level of success you may experience by following the advice and strategies contained in this book, and you accept the risk that results will differ for each individual. The examples provided in this book show exceptional results, which may not apply to the average reader, and are not intended to represent or guarantee that you will achieve the same or similar results.

Book design by:
Melvyn Paulino
melvynpaulino.com

Proofreader:
Anne-Marie George
proofmewrite101@gmail.com

I want to thank the awakened feminine and all my teachers for initiating me into sacred manhood, living my authentic purpose, and inspiring me to write this book.

TABLE OF CONTENTS

INTRODUCTION

I never imagined that one day I would coach men and women in their intimate relationships and sex-life, much less write a book that helps men understand women better and women understand themselves better.

Enduring immense personal struggles and the loss of my father led me to work on myself and to write this book. I was 15 years old when my father died in my arms, after a 3-year battle with colon cancer. For three years, I watched my father slowly become thinner and weaker each second. His death traumatized me deeply and I suffered its after effects for many years. Every day I woke up with intense anxiety and suffered from an auto-immune disease called "Neurodermatitis," which meant that I constantly had rashes and open wounds on my skin.

I hated life. I hated waking up. The only place to escape from my anxiety was to sleep or to do intense breathwork. Reading spiritual literature and practicing pranayama allowed me to release my stored trauma and to come out of my pain and suffering, but only for a while; I still felt miserable within. Breathwork helped me to regain a healthy psyche, and listening to spiritual teachers soothed my anxiety. However, I knew there was more I needed to learn; something I did not grasp yet.

Despite my great efforts to awaken and to be as "spiritual" as possible, I was entirely out of integrity in my dating life. I had no idea how to hold space for the feminine. I hit on every beautiful woman that I found on the street, prided myself in getting a woman's number, and my entire confidence was built around me dating one woman after the other. My male friends called me "Casanova."

I received constant compliments for my charisma, my charm, the way I could talk to women, yet I felt empty and depleted within. The more women I dated, the more self-judgmental I felt about my integrity levels.

I decided to shift my approach radically even before I entered my second serious relationship. Prior to the relationship, I studied various books about conscious masculinity and masculine and feminine dynamics, and was eager to use this freshly gained knowledge. I trained myself to use these teachings in my relationship and to create a safe space for my girlfriend at that time. I failed miserably at the beginning, but I kept going. I was so determined to create a deep, healthy relationship, and willing to go the extra-mile. I was on a mission, for my intimate relationship to be my training ground that would forge me into a spiritual warrior.

The relationship had many ups and downs, but it was filled with love and passion. When we broke up, we talked for one hour on the phone, cried, and thanked each other for our wonderful time together and the lessons we had learned. When I felt most heartbroken, I made the decision to become the man I have always yearned to be and this sparked a new fire within me. Sitting with my heart in meditation, I connected to my mission and purpose like never before. A new consciousness wanted to flow through me, one that felt ancient and yet like home.

I started to receive more and more clients. I did not expect such quick results but after I coached a man over a few sessions, he began to experience deep and profound sex. Another man learned to leave his toxic relationship and attracted a new, suitable partner. I posted more often on social media about intimate relationships and masculine and feminine dynamics and received hundreds of messages from people all over the world, thanking me for my service.

It felt surreal to me. I thought that everyone had access in some way to the knowledge I offered and practiced, but I quickly realized that 99% of all men and women suffer tremendously in their intimate relationships and sex-life.

Men and women would naturally come to me with their relationship and sex-related problems. People would open up to me in a way that they had never done before with anyone else, revealing intimate details and looking for solutions.

I started to receive epiphanies about the teachings I now share in my meditation practice and everyday life. I would wake up in the middle of the night and journal these radical revelations. I would look at how the sun's rays touched a woman's fragile shoulders, and it inspired and moved me to write deep poetry about the feminine. My mind could not understand women, but my heart did, and it was crystal-clear.

The nature of the feminine makes sense to me. The reason why a woman behaves the way she does makes sense to me. It is like my brain has been wired to understand intimate relationship dynamics and all the subtle nuances they entail.

I stand humbled and in awe of the source of this knowledge and the fact that it has been bestowed upon me. I therefore wrote this book with the aim to help you understand women better and experience an ecstatic and blissful relationship and sex-life. If you are a woman reading this book, diving into your own nature will allow you to gain access to your sensual goddess, or the wild woman within.

Do not rush the process of reading this book. Take it slow. Feel every chapter, and reflect upon your experiences to grasp the deeper meaning behind the words. Embodying these teachings does not mean that you will never have any issues in your intimate relationship, but it provides you with the tools to do the hard work of building a strong connection.

I have walked that path, and I can tell you that you have to earn it. It is not an easy journey; it is the journey of the awakened warrior. You will swim through the ocean of the feminine, find your way through the labyrinth of her soul, only to find that home is in your heart, home is in your own presence, and home lies in the courage and fire of your breath.

In the end, you have to ask yourself only one question, "How free do I truly want to be?" This book has the power to help you find the freedom within to no longer worry about why a woman does what she does, to not become confused or annoyed by what she says, and to radically break through all obstacles that hinder you from experiencing the best love life possible.

Lastly, remember only your heart can understand the feminine. This is not a book for your rational mind. It has been written to activate the wisdom that remains rooted deep within your heart. Remember that you already possess the power and wisdom to create a thriving relationship and to be a master in the bedroom.

Part I

THE BASICS

SHE WANTS TO
FEEL SAFE

"It is our duty as men to make women feel safe again."

Whether you want to sleep with a woman, marry a woman, or create a deep relationship, this will fail if she doesn't feel safe. Safety is the most important quality you can offer a woman because it enables her to feel fully connected to you and feel comfortable to reveal her divine feminine nature.

In all relationship dynamics, the masculine is the energetic leader. I use the word masculine because the dynamics I teach about do not exclude any sexual orientation. When two women or men are together, one will inhabit the masculine pole more, and the other will operate as the feminine pole, as we all have masculine and feminine energies within. Now in most heterosexual relationships, the man inhabits the masculine pole, but there are exceptions which are fine as long as you are truly happy. As the masculine partner, you are responsible for the creation of a safe ground where your partner can blossom and feel nurtured to reveal her full self, from the dark and destructive goddess to the goddess of light. That means you hold space for all her expressions, even the ones your mind labels as less beautiful or alluring.

If you refuse to create a safe ground for your partner, your intimate life will fail because she will not feel emotionally and spiritually connected to you. Only when you truly inhabit your authentic core, whether that is masculine or feminine, will you be able to create a blissful relationship. It's not a role you have to fulfill, it is your authentic nature, your deepest gift to life and love. Before I discuss how you make a woman feel safe, here is a deeper understanding of why it is important.

Women have been suppressed for years. They have gone through collective trauma because they were not seen as being equal to men. Women have been called witches, whores, bitches, and many other unsavory names, which has left a deep imprint on our consciousness. One example occurred in the Middle Ages, between 1580 and 1630, when an estimated 50,000 people were burned at the stake, 80% of whom were women. Almost all religions suppressed the feminine, even those commonly regarded as "holy" or innocent. In Buddhism, Christianity, Hinduism, and origins of various religions, women were suppressed. Even though much has changed in today's world, there is still an ongoing battle, such as in the Gender Pay Gap in the corporate world, and on a spiritual level, as the feminine is still suppressed by the shadow of society and in the minds of close minded individuals.

If you as a partner do not have empathy or understand where she is coming from and what she has been through, you will experience a lot of suffering, and she will not feel safe. It is not easy for a woman to trust you, and it is not easy for her to open herself up fully to you. Acknowledge it, guide her into her beautiful heart, encourage her to open up, make sure she is safe and fully protected, and then she will begin to bloom. Then, and only then, will she be able to surrender into her feminine pole.

What most men don't know is that when a woman feels truly safe, she will feel nourished with endless inspiration. The feminine has filled me with purpose, passion, and a deep yearning to serve the world with my authentic gifts as a man. Making her feel safe is a journey that will bring out the best in both of you.

So how do you make a woman feel safe? Firstly you must be fully present. "Be present" or "be in the moment" have become buzzwords in personal development and the spiritual community. Being present does not mean you are enlightened or that you experience altered states of consciousness. It simply means you are not stuck in your head, but that you inhabit your entire body. To not be stuck in your head means to be aware of your surroundings, your breath, the scents you smell, the many signs the universe offers you through ordinary everyday interactions.

When men do not practice being present, they lose themselves in porn, Netflix, or gaming. In reality what they yearn for is to feel alive, to feel their truth, to penetrate the world with their presence. Women feel safe around men who are fully present. The moment you become stuck in your head, she will detect it, and she will then be unable to open herself fully to you. I will share more about her sixth sense in a later chapter of the book.

The fastest way to become present is to connect with your breath. You cannot remain in your head while you are aware of your breath. Breathe deeply into your perineum, fill your entire stomach while you inhale, and breathe up your spine while you exhale, as you pull your stomach gently towards your spine. One of the most powerful breathwork exercises is called the Microcosmic Orbit. I will not go into detail about how it works in this book, however, you will be able to find a step by step guide online.

Each time you realize she does not feel safe, or she seems annoyed, connect with your breath instead of trying to find a solution in your mind. Your words and actions are important, but your state of presence has the deepest impact on her.

The awakened warrior's sword is presence, and he sharpens it each day through his breath, as he deeply listens to both his soul and the universe. Whenever life becomes challenging, he knows that his only shelter and shield are his sharp presence. The moment he becomes fully present, his sword cuts through all doubts, all fears, which leaves him only with his authentic truth.

You can practice presence each moment of your life, either with a partner or on your own. The more you practice being in the moment when you are on your own, the easier it will be to become present with her. Of course, financial and physical safety are elements which she values. However, your presence sits at the top of the pyramid of needs, without your presence your intimate relationship cannot be nurtured and will wither like a flower in the dark.

THE ART OF
DEEP LISTENING

When a woman expresses her deepest emotions to you, you need to just listen. No fixing. No solutions. Just pure and honest listening.

I used to be a bad listener. Instead of truly hearing a woman out, I always thought about what I would say next. This pattern kept me stuck in my head and did not allow me to pay attention to her fully. Deep listening is not about only listening to her words; it is about receiving her juicy and nourishing feminine energy. Only two things make a man truly happy: To be left alone with his purpose, and to receive a woman in all her beauty. Whenever you listen deeply to a woman, you fill your body, mind, and soul with energy. You do not listen only to her wisdom; you listen to the muse of her feminine heart, the sacred feminine flute. That is why you feel so energized when you listen deeply to a woman; your tiredness fades away and you are filled with a burning flame to live your mission.

At the beginning of a relationship is when you will most likely listen deeply; however, at some point, your old habits will resurface. Each time you do not listen deeply to a woman, you fail to receive her, and she feels disconnected from you. It creates distrust inside her and leaves your heart empty, as you yearn to receive her divine feminine energy that simultaneously cools and fires up your cells.

You need to become a full-time warrior in order to master the art of deep listening. Initially your bad habits will arise, and your shadow will not want to receive her. Men who feel unworthy often do not listen deeply. They are afraid of receiving everything a woman has to offer, including her beauty. This pattern applies to both women and men, we yearn for deep and healthy intimacy, yet when it is presented before us, our old wounds resurface and tell us that we are not worthy enough to receive it.

Deep down we are all worthy to experience true love, however, we have to do the deep inner work in order to feel that resonate deep within.

The next time you have a conversation with a woman, pay attention to your physical being. Keep your spine upright, tuck in your chin and relax your shoulders behind your chest. Keep your breath natural and relaxed, yet deeper than normal. Now, listen to her, her body, her tongue, her soft lips, and her divine essence. If you become good at this, you will receive heatwaves of her nectar and her softness, that both opens your heart and strengthens you as a man.

Her deepest fantasy is to express everything to you, through her words, her oceanic gestures and her wild energy. Whenever you listen, in order to receive her fully, you are holding space for all that she is. You create a sacred and powerful container that allows her to be fierce and wild. This creates a safe ground for her because she feels heard, comfortable with you and able to express her thoughts and feelings.

As you listen deeply to her, she starts to surrender fully. At first she will do it subtly, but after a while, you will notice how her entire nervous system becomes like a gentle ocean and she fills you with passion and deep inspiration, opening your heart to the entire universe.

WHEN A WOMAN
NEEDS SPACE

*When a woman needs space, it doesn't mean you have
failed. It means you have an opportunity to dive deep
within.*

The feminine can become like a drug. Her compliments, her
radiance, her laughter starts to fill the void you carry inside
your heart, and you become dependent. Maybe you were addicted
to porn, masturbation, or binge-watching Netflix, and now with
her those addictions seem to have disappeared. Or have they?

The truth is you have simply replaced your old addictions
with her radiant feminine energy. Her compliments, her touch,
and making love give you the illusion that you are healed. This is
a dangerous place to be because you never have any guarantees in
life.

Many men make the mistake of taking a woman for granted.
The moment she distances herself from you or needs space, the
void you have replaced with her energy gets ripped open. Suddenly, you can no longer stand your ground, you become needy and

insecure. You start to overthink everything and lose all patience and ability to stay calm.

You have zero control over her. Even if you let her go fully and continue to live your purpose, she might not come back; however, the likelihood of her return is much lower when you become needy and dependent.

I always thought that there was a magic recipe to get a woman back, or that when I fully live my truth, nothing in my personal life will go wrong. Things do not work out all the time; you will get rejected, you will fail, you will lose battles no matter how confident and awakened you are. Look at these as life's challenges that serve to strengthen a man's soul.

If she is meant to be in your life, she will return. If she is not, let her go and focus all your energy on your mission. As long as you are attached to her compliments and her radiance, you are vulnerable to great suffering. This isn't the kind of vulnerability that allows you to grow.

When a woman distances herself from you, do not chase her. It is a denial of your masculine strength and integrity. However, if you fucked up greatly, and you feel a strong desire to fight for the relationship or to share your heart with her, then go for it.

There can be many reasons why she needs space. The most common one is that she is testing your confidence and level of emotional mastery. She loves nothing more than for you to remain emotionally in control during difficult or stormy times. She distances herself from you in order to see whether you can take care of yourself and continue to move towards your deepest purpose. If you become insecure and abandon your mission because of her, your core energy is weakened and you demonstrate that she cannot fully trust you as a man.

Give her space when she needs it, and focus on doing the deep inner work on yourself. You are not here to comfort her or to keep her around you. Your job is only to serve yourself and the world and to come to her from that place of strength. Let the universe take care of everything else. She loves it when you remain focused on your priorities and unaffected when she gives you a little less attention.

Another reason for her distancing might be that she chooses to no longer be with you. While this can be brutal and painful it does not mean you have messed up. It simply means that the universe has something else in mind for you and her. Heartbreak, for both women and men, is intensely painful. It rips your heart open, leaves you empty and depressed, and you think the world will end.

But birds continue to hum, flowers continue to grow and the sun keeps shining. Everything in nature changes. The entire universe is in a constant flux, and the feminine is a manifestation of the universe.

One day, she might seem distant, and another, she might seem closer to you; do not take it too seriously. The moment you become dependent upon receiving her approval, you are already lost, and if she doesn't leave you, you will live a life of mediocrity. See it as part of your spiritual training. Women are not here to make you happy and to fill the void within but to test you over and over again in order for you to reclaim your soul's freedom. I will go in-depth about feminine testing in a later chapter.

Whether she distances herself from you or leaves completely, you feel the pain in your heart and the emptiness in your stomach. Yes it is painful, but as long as you are addicted to the feminine, and as long as you are dependent, you cannot unleash your true power. Be grateful for women who rip this wound of yours open. Do not wish for a woman to comfort you; do not wish for an easy life. Wish to be so confident and so aligned with your core's mission that nothing can bring you off center. This is the kind of freedom and liberation you were born for; it is your birthright to unleash it.

It is important for us to differentiate between the oracle of the awakened feminine and the wounded feminine. When a woman is trapped in her trauma and pulls away when you express how much you love her, then comes back into your life when you pull away, it has nothing to do with the awakened feminine. An awakened woman would never distance herself from you when you show up with your full heart and live your mission.

HER ANGER

When a woman becomes very angry at you it's a clear sign that you are avoiding an important piece of your life. It might be your emotions, your mission or your capacity to serve as a masculine presence. Her anger is a way to say, "Get your shit together. I want to feel you. I yearn for your presence. Get off the couch and penetrate the world with your deep consciousness."

A woman's natural state of being is one of ecstasy and flow. When she is angry with you do not ask why; it does not matter, it is more important that you listen to her thoughts and feelings as she reports them. Feminine anger has unfortunately been deeply suppressed by society. Due to the conditioning men have received about feminine anger, they lack the skills to deal with it, and collapse into fear or panic once they are met by its fierce nature. When a woman gets angry it is often labeled "unsexy" or "too masculine", which is a knee jerk reaction that loses out on learning about the reason behind the emotion. Questioning her will only increase her anger. So what should you do?

Do not try to fix her anger and solve her problems before you understand and listen to her fully. Offer her solutions only if she asks for it, and only after you listen to her. Many men play the role of a therapist, which creates unwanted sexual neutrality that keeps you stuck in a negative pattern. For instance when you argue, it slowly erodes the trust you have accumulated from the beginning. Without trust, intimacy cannot flower. Do not think about her anger and do not label it; simply breathe deeply into your balls and meet her with an alert compassion. She craves to be accepted and embraced. If you become irritated and collapse into fear when she shares this strong emotion with you, she will become increasingly too angry to lead you towards reclamation of your true inner freedom.

SHE DOESN'T WANT TO BE YOUR NUMBER ONE

A woman isn't interested in being your number one priority. What she truly longs for is for you to harness your masculine presence, slay dragons, work on yourself and live your authentic truth. Even if she would never admit it, deep down, she goes wild when you choose your mission before her.

A friend once told me that a man answers firstly to the universe, secondly to his heart and thirdly to his woman. The universe fills you with your divine mission and your heart allows you to align with it. Your woman will test you to see if you answer to both the universe and your heart.

It often seems as if she wants to be your number one priority. She might tell you, "Spend more time with me; give me more attention," yet deep down, she only wants you to say, "I love you baby, but I have a mission to fulfill." Although she might seem disappointed, she is highly attracted to your relentless commitment and yearning for your deepest freedom. She might even get angry with you, however, she feels fully met and penetrated by your level of emotional mastery.

Women long for connection and men yearn for freedom. If you choose at any point intimacy or sex over your desire for freedom, you limit yourself greatly because you did not choose from your deepest core; you allowed your mind to fool you.

SHE WANTS
TO BE LED

*In today's world, women have become very independent
and that is a good thing. Women no longer have to bow to
the voice of hurt little boys. However, on a deeper level,
the feminine still wants to be led by the masculine.*

Notice how soft and fragile she becomes when you center
yourself in your strength and lead courageously from your
heart. Notice how playful and innocent her actions become,
which in turn fuel you with deep inspiration and refresh your five
senses.

As the awakened man it is your responsibility to lead, whether it be in conversations, the relationship or the bedroom. She
wants to be as untamed and unpredictable as the ocean, therefore
you must become a great captain of your ship, as you sail into this
vast territory. You are mission-driven; you cannot breathe proper-
ly as a man if you do not possess a sense of direction and recognize
your goals in life. You don't need full clarity around what it is exactly you have to do in the world. But remember that what truly
matters is finding your unique mission.

Break through the walls of the people pleaser inside you and tell your shadow to fuck off, as you become the leader you were born to be. It is in your nature to lead, to sail into the endless ocean and to be willing to die in your pursuit. If you are afraid to lead, and if you need a woman to validate you and tell you that you are a good boy, your intimate life will be deprived of depth and attraction. You will swim in a sea of self-pity and worry, and drown in your own fears. Breathe deeply. Get to know who you truly are. Honor the warrior and king inside you. Speak greatly about yourself. Then become the leader you were born to be.

STOP TRYING TO FIX HER

Whenever you try to fix a woman, you deny her feminine nature. She doesn't want a therapist or coach; the only thing she wants is your undivided attention. Your presence allows her to surrender into bliss and bloom like a wildflower.

If you are like most men, you probably try to fix a woman when she becomes very emotional or irritated. Your intention comes from a good place; you think that solutions will help her to get rid of her challenges, as it does for you. However, women think differently. As a man, you solve most problems through analysis and rational thought. Women do not usually solve problems that way.

Whenever you play the coach, the therapist, or simply offer solutions that you genuinely think will work, it will make her feel unsafe and her heart will start to contract. She does not want to be fixed by you because she will not feel listened to and heard; you will give her the impression that you find her inadequate and do not respect her thoughts and feelings enough to truly grasp her perspective.

All she wants is your undivided and authentic presence. She wants to feel how you show up as a liberated man, and only then can she soften and relax again.

Pay attention the next time she seems annoyed by your tendency to fix her. Do not look for solutions from your own perspective; she is not a car that has to be fixed by you. Instead, trust your ability to lead consciously and to be fully present.

Part 2

THE FEMININE ORACLE

THE TESTING
WILL NEVER STOP

The reason why a woman tests you repeatedly is because she yearns for your most awakened Self. She does not want to settle for anything else but your deepest truth. The resistance you feel towards her wild and unpredictable tests is the fire that forges you into a spiritual warrior.

The mediocre man within you does not want to be tested. He wants to remain in his comfort zone and live a simple life consisting great sex, a decent job, a couple of good friends and minimal or no interest in spiritual work. While it may seem that this life makes you happy, I can guarantee you that all men who are stuck in a mediocre life yearn for more. Mediocrity is not attractive to women, and it only serves to weaken you. Deep down, the mediocre man knows he has more potential and could do better, yet he chooses the easy, safe path.

The awakened man within you loves to be tested. He finds a woman's testing sexy and divine. Women are better than any therapist or coach in identifying your blind-spots and exposing how and where in life you bullshit yourself. Every time you notice that her testing annoys you, let it be a reminder that you are probably stuck in a personal comfort zone. Approach her testing as a chance to enliven your spirit as you love to be challenged in your presence and depth as a man.

The more awakened a woman is, the more she will test you in ways that make absolutely no sense to your rational mind, as a means to refine you and to gauge your loyalty to your mission. These tests are born from a higher consciousness, and provide you an opportunity to experience breathtaking breakthroughs in your spiritual journey, if you allow her tests to sharpen and guide you.

She might say one thing but mean another because she wants you to remain truthful to your intuition and what you sense in your body. She might change her mind abruptly, just to see how rooted and grounded you can remain. She might remind you of past mistakes during times of hardship, to determine whether you demonstrate wisdom and resilience during a crisis or fall back into unconscious behavior.

At her deepest core, she is helping you to remain conscious at all times and to keep you aligned with your mission. The number one priority of the awakened man or the warrior of the heart, is to remain conscious and present when your heart wants to close due to the anxiety of being triggered.

You will be unable to relax into your comfort zone with a highly awakened woman; the only way to feel truly free is to calmly face the fire of her constant testing and to trust yourself no matter what happens. Once you lean into her testing and befriend the sharpening of your sword, your training as a spiritual warrior, you will want nothing more than for her to be her own unique self. You will find freedom in her mood swings, and home in her unpredictability. You will realize that what your mind despises is in reality what your heart desires because you wish to be challenged and to have impetus to grow.

WHY SHE LOVES
TO SAY MAYBE

A feminine woman loves to say "maybe." She loves to be as a leaf, as she dances in the wind and creates a cosmic and divine mess. Her maybe is an invitation for you to bring leadership and direction into the intimate relationship.

You have probably already noticed that a woman loves to say "maybe" or "I don't know." Most men will respond "Be more clear!" or "Figure your life out!" However, the moment you tell her to be clearer, what you actually do is to discount her feelings and miss a powerful opportunity to create immense attraction and intimacy. She does not say these things because she has not figured out what she wants; she says them because she wants to feel your depth of clarity and conscious leadership in each moment.

Whenever you notice that you resent her or become annoyed by her "lack of clarity," you are probably projecting your lack of confidence on her. An awakened man understands when a woman invites him to step up and to direct the intimate relationship. Make it a conscious practice to spot an invitation to penetrate her with your clarity and decisiveness. This is a wonderful opportunity to experience deeper intimacy with a woman.

The next time you ask her something and she says "maybe", or she comes to you about an important decision she is unable to resolve, penetrate through her lack of clarity with your deep masculine decisiveness. You do not decide for her, but you offer your greatest leadership qualities and tell her without hesitation what needs to be done. Remember, an awakened woman does not do this because she needs your clarity; she does it because she wants you to grow into the most powerful man the universe has ever known.

HER GUARD

The calmer and more relaxed you are, the more a woman lets her guard down and becomes able to trust you.

Every woman has the protective instinct to guard her heart, but deep intimacy is born when your energy and authenticity causes her to drop her guard. When this mantle is cast off, she will long to tear off her clothes and press her soft cheeks against your strong and warming chest. But none of this is possible if you blame her, attempt to fix her, or get stuck in your head. Her guard guides you towards freedom and true liberation because it prompts you to embrace all that life offers with an open heart. To open your heart to the beauty of the world is fairly easy, compared to opening it to challenge, struggle and moments of doubt and internal collapse. Her guard might come up during sex, in a heated argument, or in everyday moments. As the masculine partner you have the gift to hold space for her tender heart and become a friend to her guard. This frees you, carrying you further on your journey to becoming a better man.

A mediocre man will avoid the challenge and try to avoid befriending a woman's guard. An awakened man, however, will face her guard with an open heart. It might prove challenging, yet a man only grows through challenge, and deep down loves the struggle of softening her heart and creating a sacred space for her.

Remember, women have been suppressed for centuries and while times have changed, this repression still carries on unchallenged by the subconscious minds of many. For this reason, getting angry at her guard will not help; rather you should accept the manner in which she seeks to protect herself. Befriend her guard with your compassion and dedication and make her feel safe in your kingdom.

DO YOU HAVE A
CONTROL ISSUE?

A woman's untamable nature will often trigger control issues in a man. Allow her wild spirit to tear your shadow self apart, as you fiercely embrace the side of you that needs to be in control.

I magine you are dating a wonderful woman with whom you get along. Your conversations are passionate and deep. Having sex with her feels like union with the universe. Everything seems perfect with no need to doubt any aspect of this connection. You are perplexed when suddenly, her behavior changes. She becomes more distant. Her text messages become brief, and her responses are further apart. She does not shower you with compliments as before, and tiny matters annoy her.

When you have control issues, you begin to overthink every aspect of your experience. As a result, you are no longer grounded, your rational mind wastes time trying to fix the perceived problems and find solutions. You find yourself asking her questions rooted in insecurity such as, "Do you still love me," or "Do you still like me?" This is not how deep intimacy works. Your constant grasping to control her is always a sign that you are anxious to lose her, and it will drive her further away. Your mind will struggle to understand what transpired. Everything seemed perfect before, but now you question if that was reality or a fiction you invented.

Almost every man has found himself in a similar situation, coming to the realization that the relationship was not perfect. It was built on a fragile basis. And the reason is because at some point, you entered the comfort zone and no longer took risks or expressed yourself boldly.

You started to enjoy the soft pillows, the romantic movies and the cuddling a little too much, more than the pursuit of your goals and mission, and stopped the ongoing challenge to become the best version of yourself.

If you remember one thing from this book, it is this: You cannot own a woman. She is never yours; she belongs to herself. She might want to be with you, but that can change at any time. The moment you make yourself dependent on her choosing you, you suffer and lose your authentic core because you rely more on her than on your own goals.

When she pulls away, let this remind you to "get your shit together." You might want to take a journal and reflect about where you are, in terms of an area you currently ignore in your life. It might be your mission, finances, creating deep intimacy, or challenging yourself through spiritual and growth work.

Obviously, it is not black and white; she might pull away because she is stressed out or dealing with her own challenges. It is up to you to delve into your heart and act accordingly. Deep down you know whether you sell yourself short or not. When she pulls away and you are utilizing your strength, do not worry; she will soften and relax soon enough through your calm and grounded energy.

FEMININE STORMS

When a woman becomes very emotional, penetrate her
with your deep presence. If she talks fast, talk slowly.
If she moves a lot, remain still. Meet her as a deep and
grounded man, not as a little boy.

P art of embodying the awakened man is to learn how to remain grounded when a woman unleashes her furious, wild,
and oceanic storm. However, most men have no idea how to han-
dle a woman when she talks fast, her movements become unpredictable, and her breath becomes wild. Breathe deeply into your
cock and balls. Imagine your feet being rooted into the earth. Allow your gaze to be sharp and fierce.

Let your speech and movements be born from your heart,
from your depth, and your authentic core. It is not about deliver-
ing a script or trying to soothe her emotions because she will
think you are trying to invalidate them which only serves to frus-
trate her. Let her storms be an invitation for you to just be. Feel
and experience yourself as free, unwavering consciousness, and a
liberated man with strong balls, who is rooted into the earth like

a tree. A man who does not collapse when faced with feminine storms is a powerful man because, when you can stand your ground with an unpredictable woman who unleashes her wild and divine chaos on you, you prove that you can truly face life's challenges with dignity and grace.

WHEN SHE FRIENDZONES YOU

> *If you become friendzoned by a woman, it means you did not express your needs. You will face this lesson over and over again until you own who you are, your needs, your desires, and your mission.*

She does not desire to friendzone you, but she has to if you are a pleaser and do not express your needs. The feminine is like the universe, and it tests you where you need it most. It is a blessing to become friendzoned because it gives you the opportunity to work on your ability to own who you are and to express your desires clearly. Men who get friendzoned repeatedly lack clarity and the courage to express it. If you want her, tell her. Show her. Express your desires. She loves your mission-driven spirit and decisiveness.

Own who you are and each inch of your soul. Own your shortcomings, your failures, your mission, your heart, your needs, and your values. When a man owns who he is, his stance becomes one of a powerful king and a fierce warrior. Own your desires, and you will never get friendzoned again.

You have to be willing to risk losing her by expressing your deep desires. The moment you compromise to "just be friends for now" it means you lack confidence and played a part in building a shaky foundation. No matter how much she likes you, 99% of the time she will feel distrust when you suddenly share your true feelings and desires with her. Think about it, you basically lied to her, so how can she trust you? You have just shown her that you are not trustworthy, and deep in her subconscious she might think, "what if he lies to me or changes his mind again when we go through a challenging time together?"

HER DEEPEST
DESIRE

A woman's deepest desire is to become like an untamable ocean and an erupting volcano, so unpredictable that only the openness of your heart can hold space for her.

She is done being a predictable, well-behaved woman. She hates all labels and all that limits her from fully expressing her desires. She wants to erupt, to become so wild that her furious flames start to burn down everything that stands in her way.

In order to truly connect with the feminine, you must accept her in her pure state and in her wildness. Breathe deeply, and maintain strong posture. Become a source of masculine strength and energy and receive her in all of her glory. As you meet her in the chaos, stand there like few would dare. As she unleashes all her wildness on you, you suddenly connect to the source of all your masculine strength. You enter a state of being, where no thoughts and emotions can meet you. Then you laugh. You laugh because you burn in her flames, yet your depth and strength pervade all of her and all around you.

You hold her fiercely in the flames, but you are still full of compassion and burning love. The fire starts to change its color. Your depth transforms everything, and she enters a state of pure bliss and ecstasy, as you become one with the earth. True intimacy is born in this mysterious place. Only those who are willing to slay dragons and surrender to their shadow are able to create deep intimacy because they have fought for it with their masculine strength.

Your mind does not understand this place, only your heart will know instinctively what to do. This place is the erosion of masculine and feminine energy, where Shiva and Shakti meet and unleash who they truly are, without labels, conditioning, or thoughts.

You will not be able to go there all the time, obviously, as we all deal with conditioning, trauma, triggers, and pain. It is not about trying to achieve a peak; it is about having small moments of eternal bliss, high ecstasy, and realizing our true essence. If you are able to go to this place just once, it will entirely shift how the feminine responds to you. You might become stuck in your head again, and lose yourself in worry and fear, but once you have discovered it you will never lose access to the depth that always rests inside you, as it waits to become unleashed.

THE DIVINE MIRROR

The divine feminine is the rawest, wildest, most honest mirror you will ever encounter. While the coward runs and hides behind illusions, the awakened man opens his heart and goes into battle. He will tame dragons and face his deepest shadows, since he knows that deep within, her heart will guide him home.

A woman is a reflection of your state of consciousness. Whenever you become stuck in your mind or worry, she will mirror your sentiments. The more a woman is in touch with her divine feminine, the more she will mirror your pain, wounds, and the places where you lack integrity. The more a man becomes stuck in his head, the less a divine mirror will make sense to him. He will blame every woman who reflects his pain, and he will project his insecurities onto her, then defend his life of mediocrity.

This happens due to a protection mechanism of his heart. His heart is guarded by walls of steel so every time he meets himself in the divine feminine mirror, his walls come up and his heart shuts down.

It is painful for a man to reconnect with his heart, and to tear the walls down, but it is much more painful for him to remain stuck in his head. The mind is a powerful tool, but making it your home, will drain you and leave you empty. The antidote to this is meeting the depth of your being in the raw mirror of a woman. Instead of becoming triggered by her, move inwards, and face the shadows that you try to avoid.

She does not reflect your consciousness on purpose; she does this instinctively because she wants you to become the freest, most authentic and awakened version of yourself. Honor the divine mirror, and you will meet your deepest Self in the naked rawness of her reflection.

When your deepest shadow emerges, do not run, do not hide, and do not project. Sit with it. Breathe into it until it dissolves. Feel into your suppressed anger, the dark codependency, and your tendency to control or fix the feminine. Be with it until your presence slaughters every last inch of your shadow that seeks to control her, in this brutal battle of consciousness.

HER GREATEST GIFT

*The greatest gift a woman can give a man is to guide him
out of his ego and back into his heart.*

The way she moves her body, the way she dances, and the way
her hips make love to the ether and the sky, shatter your ego.
Her divine nectars unspool on your longing tongue, and you will
feel the embrace of her ancient womb, as she rips your chest open
and reveals the conscious lover within you.

When you lay your eyes on her tender shoulders and her naked fragility, you cannot help but feel the strength of your cock
and devote yourself to the path of truth, the path of devotion, the
path of naked awareness, and your samurai-sharp consciousness.
Let her rip your ego apart. Drink her liquids like the fountain of
youth. Fuck your way into heaven, into supreme softness, and
your heart's truth and courage will set the world on fire.

HER SIXTH SENSE

A woman has a sixth sense when it comes to knowing whether you are present or stuck in your head.

You might have noticed that women become irritated out of nowhere. Suddenly, she no longer smiles at your jokes and her entire vibe makes you think, "What the fuck is going on here?"

A woman can instinctively feel when you become stuck in your head, and she will demonstrate this to you when she is in touch with her feminine energy. She will do this in a very subtle way; it is rare that a woman will directly tell you that you are not present enough, because deep down, she becomes turned on when you figure it out and ground yourself again.

You might ask her, "What is going on?" but most of the time, she will be unable to respond as she will not know the answer herself, it is her deeply rooted intuition that provides her the signal. This doesn't mean that you are responsible for her mood, however; it can indicate that you have not shown up as your most authentic version.

Deep down, she wants you to become your most enlightened Self. She wants to feel Shiva, the destroyer of illusions, and your all-pervading presence and depth. When you shift your mindset from, "Why is she acting that way again" to "This is an opportunity for me to become present," everything changes.

HER PERIOD

When a woman goes through her period, you have an opportunity to train your spiritual muscle and to sharpen your presence and your confidence. She might test you, however, deep down, she hopes that you remain centered and strong. Passing a woman's test by being there for her during her period will make her horny at a Greek Goddess level.

A woman in her period is so soft and fragile. She yearns for your deep presence as the sacred protector of the earth and her heart. Giving in to her moods will only make her more irritated and weaken your masculine core. Having no empathy will make her feel lonely and disconnected from your heart. You should be a fierce, heartful warrior. Be there for her, but set boundaries. She will love it when you do not give in to her moods. If she tests you more when she is on her period, remain calm; it means nothing. Your authentic core knows exactly how to respond to her.

Say for instance, she complains about the world and her life. What you should do first is look deep into her eyes and breathe into your strong cock. After a while, press her body gently against yours. Within seconds, you will find that her energy shifts and spontaneous joy arises. Smile to yourself as you appreciate the forever changing rhythm of a woman.

Another important note is that you should not analyze the actions of a woman in her period. Let her be the furious ocean, the calm ocean, and everything in between. Remain focused on your breath and deepest mission. Use the time of her period to become a more confident and unshakable man. Her period is like a sign from the universe which asks you to go deeper to find calm and peace in the storm.

SACRED MYSTERY

The more you try to understand a woman with your mind, the less you allow your heart to expand into the sacred mystery of her soul.

Stop trying to understand women. There is nothing to understand; there is nothing to grasp. There is only what you feel, embrace and receive. Most men spend their entire life overthinking things such as, "Why did she say this? Why did she change her mind? Why did she lose interest in me?" This is a complete waste of your time. Your ego tries to hinder you from comprehending the bigger picture and the deeper truth. At the deepest level, there is nothing to understand, nothing to fix, and nothing to change. All of this is part of the divine orchestration of the universe, and so are women.

Her mysterious nature is an invitation to become fiercely present and to stop trying to control her or anything in her life. She is like the soft fine sand of the Sahara. The moment you try to hold on to it, it runs through your fingers, and becomes forever lost in the dunes. Fuck your mind and become so present that your thoughts no longer govern your depth of consciousness. Meet her from this place, and you will see her positive reaction.

Part 3

THE SACRED DANCE

PATIENCE

Nothing is more attractive to a woman than patience,
and nothing is more unattractive than to rush things.

I used to rush through life, and I thought of each moment as a means to an end, but that kind of lifestyle repels a woman. As you have probably already noticed, a woman's feelings are unpredictable. You have passionate sex, and suddenly, she becomes triggered by something you said. You have an amazing evening together, yet a little while afterwards she seems distant and cold. Most of the time, she does this instinctively because she wants to feel your depth of patience. Most men become triggered by this unpredictability and ask themselves if there is an uncomplicated woman out there.

You do not want an easy woman. Her testing, at least to some degree, attracts you and sharpens your masculine qualities, as it allows you to push beyond your self-imposed limitations and become who you truly are. A man with a very masculine core needs to constantly stretch beyond his comfort zone, or he will feel useless and not in service to the world. You do not transcend your current limitations to appear cool; you transcend them in order to unleash the fire of your soul onto the world and to leave a legacy in this world.

Bring patience into the bedroom, as well as in everyday conversations with her, and do not become irritated when she tests you. She does this because she feels safe around you.

One of the most common examples is that a woman will test your patience by bringing things up at the worst possible time. You might be stuck in traffic, or late to an appointment, and suddenly, she wants to discuss something important. It is easy to lash out during those moments, and while you should definitely set boundaries, it might feel difficult to remain patient and calm. Find calm within yourself even when it proves incredibly difficult, and she will appreciate your strength.

DON'T TELL HER YOUR PROBLEMS

*When you become intimate with a woman and open
your heart it is easy to fall into the trap of seeing her
as someone who can save you from your internal and
external challenges. While it is important to be vulnerable
and share your heart's truth with her, you ruin the
attraction, trust, and love if you depend on her for
solutions in the hope she can help you figure out your life.*

There is a big difference between being vulnerable and being a sensitive, touchy, new-age guy. A man who is vulnerable will open his heart and express his grief or pain to a woman, but he will not hope for her to fix his life. The sensitive, touchy new-age guy utilizes vulnerability to lean on a woman, and he recreates the bond he had, or never had, with his mother. The sensitive, touchy new-age guy is found in hippie communities, smoking joints, wearing clothes with chakras on it, and talking about oneness and God while he is possessed by a cowardly, anxious shadow. I used to be that guy, apart from wearing hippie clothes and smoking joints. And I felt miserable because the touchy new-age guy has no conscious access to his masculine fierceness, and feels weak and less in sync with his mission and purpose in life.

You can share everything with a woman if you maintain some awareness of how you share it. If you begin to collapse, lose your ground, and become stuck in a story or drama, it will repel her and make her trust you less. If you share from your heart, even if you feel intense pain, you must maintain some level of control inside you. This is not about controlling your tears. Crying is freeing and important, and she will love your tears, as long as you do not break down in tears all the time.

What this means is that you can express yourself the way you are, but ensure you remain grounded and do not become overwhelmed by your situation.

The wisdom lies in maintaining your depth and integrity, even in the midst of challenging emotions. If you lose it, she will lose it as well, since she is your divine mirror.

You do not have to be perfect. You can possess immense grief, pain, and shadows; however, you can express them to her in a vulnerable manner, without losing your ground and natural confidence. It is often wiser to move inwards and sit for a while with your pain, in lieu of sharing everything that pops up in your head. Ask yourself the simple question, "Is this really important right now? Am I expressing what I truly feel?"

She wants your full clarity. If you feel strong grief, tell her. If you feel unworthiness, tell her. If you feel intimidated by her power, tell her. Do not tell her in the hope that she will give you a solution or help you out of it. Tell her from a state of, "This is what I am going through; I love you, and I am going to deal with it."

She loves when you take care of your internal and external challenges because she treasures the heart warrior inside you. What she wants is a man that recognizes a challenge and goes into battle with all his heart and soul.

You might have realized that a woman always comes to you with her problems. She loves to tell you about what she is going through. She loves to feel your presence, when you listen deeply to her, in lieu of trying to fix or change her.

Share your heart's desires with her. Get fucking real with her, and be yourself. Be raw and honest. The moment you realize you depend too much on a woman and look to her for answers, let go. She is not here to lead you to some truth outside yourself; she is here to lead you into your own heart and truth, through her constant testing.

PRAISE HER

*When you praise a woman, her breath becomes soft, her
body relaxes, and her heart radiates pure and loving
feminine energy. As you receive her radiance, your heart
will roar in victory.*

This is not to say that a man does not like compliments or
praise; it means a woman is able to grow at the deepest level
when she feels supported and nurtured.

When a woman deeply opens herself to you, she feels sensitive
towards blame, projections, and criticism. If you do not praise
her, hold space for her, and create an environment where she feels
safe, then you deny her feminine radiance and her offering to the
universe.

Do not merely tell her how beautiful she is; praise her subtle
qualities such as her sensual heart, her fragile shoulders, her tender spine, her softness, and her open vulva. This appreciative form
of praise is so powerful because it is unique and truly authentic. It
is the opposite of our dating and pick-up line culture because it is
chivalrous and permits immense depth of appreciation.

BECOME A
MOUNTAIN

The feminine is like the ocean: forever changing and untamable, yet its depth remains the same. The masculine is like a mountain; it is still, calm, and grounded in its own roots.

There is a divine dance going on between her feminine energy, Shakti, and your masculine energy, Shiva. This dance creates immense attraction and a longing for each other on all levels: mind, body, and soul. When people fall out of love, they have simply stopped dancing or building a relationship together. This dance determines whether you experience mind-blowing sex and deep trust, or great suffering in your relationship. Understanding how to dance and build a relationship is everything, if you want to create deep intimacy. The teachings of this book are all you need.

Whenever she experiences intense emotions, whenever she tests you, she invites you to become a mountain. You can imagine being a mountain with roots that dig deep into the earth. She can test you in every way she wants, and she can throw anything at you, but you must remain calm, grounded, and still as a rock, as you carry great depth within.

I used to collapse whenever a woman experienced intense emotions. The moment you lose your stance as a mountain, you block the flow of intimacy in the relationship, as well as the natural attraction between you. It is not natural to experience these blockages, yet when you look around at the world, you find that almost all intimate relationships do.

Men have never been taught to stand their ground. Many of us have become like the weather, and like women, we become forever changing and unpredictable.

While unpredictability is an attractive facet of a woman's nature, it weakens a man on every level. Deep within, you want to become a mountain. You want to stand your ground. You want to be still and rooted into the earth, and simply receive a woman, without any judgements and thoughts spinning inside your head.

Each time you lose your ground and start to collapse, remember your true nature as a mountain. Imagine yourself being tall, rooted into the earth, completely still, and ready to embrace the feminine even in the most terrifying storms.

GUIDE HER INTO HER HEART

The masculine gift is to guide a woman into her naked heart, and guard her while she opens like a flower.

Most women have never experienced a man who is able to guide her into her own heart, who allows her to fully surrender, and to taste the nectar of her feminine essence. That is because most men are stuck in their head and in their conditioning, and this entails a life that does not serve their heart.

Only when you no longer identify with your thoughts and emotions, and experience yourself as free consciousness and pure nothingness, can you guide a woman into her heart. You are no longer a man with a body, but you are a pure awareness that holds space for her, the ground underneath her feet, and the air that fills her lungs.

This is why meditation, breathwork, and yoga are so essential for a man to realize who he is beyond his achievements and five senses. It is so easy to become stuck in material things. The awakened man spends time every single day in deep meditation and contemplates his soul's existence. If you meditate every time you feel triggered and your heart closes, with the purpose of becoming more in sync with yourself and the present moment, you will become the man you have always yearned to be.

HOW TO TURN HER ON

> *If you really want to turn a woman on, then do the inner work. Face your fears. Sit with your heart. Train your breath. Connect to your authentic purpose.*

When you face your fears and do the inner work, she starts to soften and surrender because the warrior in you makes her feel safe. When you sit with your heart, every cell in her body starts to move in harmony with the universe. As your heart expands, so does her radiance and elegance. When you train your breath, she can feel your depth. When you breathe deeply into your pelvic floor while you make love to her, she will feel a loving explosion inside her heart.

Your authentic purpose resembles a ship that sails into the endless ocean with a clear direction, ready to overcome the most terrifying storms. She loves to stand naked on your ship and feel the ocean melting with her tender body.

There are many dating and relationship coaches out there who will try to sell you recipes and fancy techniques. There might be some value in that, but it lacks depth and authenticity. Fuck the recipes, the special techniques, the hacks. Go deep into your truth, become your own best friend, let life be your muse, and you will turn on every fiber in her soul. This is the authentic path of the awakened warrior. You do not need to change yourself or acquire some superficial techniques. Ensure you travel so deep into your truth, and follow your heart so relentlessly, that the feminine cannot help but get wet by your simple presence.

SHE LOVES
YOUR CLARITY

In order to make a woman feel safe, you need clarity in your speech and actions. Vague sentences and half-present actions show her that you have no command over your actions and are afraid to take responsibility.

Presence is not about constant clarity; no one has that. It is about knowing where you want to go, your values, your virtues, and who you are as a man. If you are not clear about where you want to go in life and what you want to do, she will subconsciously start to think that you are not strong or conscious enough to be the energetic leader, and she will lose interest, or get annoyed due to your lack of direction.

If you remain unconscious, she will gain full control over your emotions. When she wants something, you jump up, ready to leave even your deepest mission behind to please her. She tests you instinctively so that you take life by the balls and become the leader you were born to be. You might be in the middle of an important project, and she tells you that the trash has to be thrown away. If you jump up and do it immediately, she will know where your priorities lie. Instead, you gently let her know that you will deal with it once you finish your project. This will make her feel incredibly safe because she will realize that you put your mission first.

She will test you by trying to control your emotional state, and at the same time, she subconsciously hopes that you stand your ground, no matter what. This is a specifically harsh lesson for sensitive men with very low self-esteem. If you realize a woman has a deep impact on your life, and influences you easily, so much so that you collapse into fear when she does not react the way you want to, please seriously consider doing the deep inner work.

LEARN WHEN
TO SHUT UP

A man that talks like an endless waterfall will bore a woman and make her feel unsafe. When you realize that you have been talking for a long time, pause for a second, breathe deeply into your stomach, and feel into her. She loves when you slow down and intentionally create an emotional connection with her. You must be willing to receive and feel her fully and be sensitive to her needs. And that turns her on at the deepest level.

Personally, I love to talk. There is nothing wrong with enjoying communication and the sharing of experiences. It is all about balance and being sensitive to her body, her breath, and her energy. When you forget and are no longer able to give her space to be, you lose awareness of your masculine pole. When you intentionally slow down in your speech, and feel into her, you create safety for her. Without feeling safe, a woman cannot open herself towards deep intimacy.

Make this an ongoing practice. It is a practice that will create more trust, safety, and erotic friction. Whenever you notice that you have lost awareness of holding space as consciousness, simply drop into your breath and restore order. She might not consciously know what you are doing, but she will love it.

WALK THE TALK

*A man who lives by his words is magnetic
to a woman.*

Many men are strong communicators. They know how to make a woman feel seen and safe with words. Although this seems incredible, it has often been misused and contributed to the collective pain of women because these men take advantage of their knowledge. Lacking integrity is the worst position for a man. Men who do not live by their words become insecure, anxious and unsafe in their bodies. Remember: Your words have power. Your conscious speech, if fused with your heart, is magnetic to the feminine.

Do not speak insincerely to a woman. Do not make promises you will not fulfill. Remain in your highest integrity by being very conscious of your speech, and even more importantly, live by it, and follow through with your words. This requires continuous practice, but it proves worthwhile because it improves your self-esteem, and in turn, women feel much safer in your presence.

SLOW DOWN

Women love it when you slow down. Slow down your speech, your breath, and your cock. It allows you to drop into your authentic presence, and will make a woman feel safe beyond her deepest desires.

Slowing down proves difficult for a man because men are always on the search for freedom. You desperately want to achieve your goals, and get to the next moment as quickly as possible; you entirely forget to be present in this moment.

Slowing down is a sign of maturity and mastery. You do not fall for the many stories your mind creates, or the momentum of your fears, and you choose to be in control, no matter how stressful life becomes. This will permit you to access your deepest intuition, to become aware of your body, breath, and your emotions. Slowing down again and again when you are stuck in your head, is crucial to mastering your habitual reactions to life.

A woman loves it when you slow down your speech; it creates safety and trust. Slowing down your breath deepens your presence and your presence creates intimacy. Lastly, slowing down your cock while you make love to a woman allows you both to experience more bliss, as you enter a world far removed from the everyday hustle of modern life.

Part 4

SEX

HER BODY

The body of a woman is like a sacred temple. Her womb is a universe on its own. Her vagina is a portal through which the sensual nectar of love flows. Her breasts are the expression of mother nature, selflessly nurturing. When you see a woman's body for what it is, you will experience intimacy at the deepest level.

Porn has brainwashed us. Many men have lost the ability to see a woman's body for what it truly is. Her body is so sacred that it should shake your deepest core and inspire you to move mountains, write poetry, create art, and live your deepest truth. When you shift out of the porn mindset you see that her vagina is an entrance into paradise. Her thighs become soft valleys, her spine becomes a rooted tree, her breasts fill you with warmth and tenderness, and the arch of her lower back symbolizes a coast gently shaped by the sea. She wants to become your muse and enjoys when you feel inspired by her body, her breath, her voice, and her feminine energy.

The only way to see her body as a sacred temple is to stop watching porn and stop engaging entirely with everything that does not represent deep intimacy. This includes one-night stands, having sex while you are drunk, and chasing women only to strengthen your ego. All of that keeps you stuck in the largely artificial porn-focused mindset. Once you transcend that mentality, you feel a healthy disgust towards it because you see through the bullshit. You understand that what once turned you on is only a shadow, merely eroticized pain, that keeps intimate relationships stuck in dysfunctional patterns.

HER WILD SIDE

A woman will not reveal her wild side in the bedroom if you do not know how to hold space for her; however, the moment she can feel your unwavering and penetrating presence, her heart opens and the wild woman is born.

Men have never been taught how to hold space for a woman and to be authentically present. A woman can directly feel when you have expectations of how she must perform in the bedroom and if you are stuck in your head. The moment you are acting from a script and need her to fit into it, there is no space for deep intimacy to flower. It is impossible to experience boredom in the bedroom if you know how to hold space and penetrate her with your unwavering presence.

That means you are fully in the moment, connected to your emotional body, and sensitive to her energy. You are both rooted within and deeply enjoying the experience, and at the same time, you can feel her heart. This requires training. Watching porn and wanking is not enough to become a master in the bedroom. It requires relentless commitment to train yourself to become more present and open to your heart and to hers.

Some men do not want to hear this and in fact may feel triggered, and I know why. It is because they desire the easy way out. But there is no easy way because men are born for the difficult path where they face one obstacle after another that can only be overcome with courage and fire.

LET HER INVITE YOU

> A man can either tell a woman that he wants to have sex with her, or he can create an environment where she invites him herself.

A woman is most attracted to a man who is in control of his sexual urges and does not need to fuck to feel intimacy. The more you can control yourself and remain grounded, the more the sexual heat between you and her will start to build up. If you are able to build up your presence, purpose, and devotion gradually, then she will simply jump on you and tell you to ravish her. A woman becomes turned on by patience. She loves the subtle dance between Shiva and Shakti, including all the little moments where you breathe in her sexual energy and do not directly act upon it.

Remain rooted in your balls and feet, and wait patiently until she invites you. The sex will prove deeper and more fulfilling because the attraction and dance is at its sacred peak. If she does not invite you, let it go. Focus on your purpose, your divine mission, and trust in your natural depth and confidence. You are not here to worry about a woman who does not want to sleep with you. You are here to offer your heart to the world.

PENETRATE
ALL OF HER

*Do not just penetrate her vagina. Make love to her eyes,
her unbreakable heart, and her tender soul.*

Anybody can put it in and fuck. There is nothing special
about that. What a woman truly craves is that you penetrate all of her, on an emotional level, while you are deep inside
her vagina. When you are inside her, feel your heart radiate into
her body. Devote yourself fully to opening her with your masculine gifts. There is no end to the ways in which she can open up to
you, and that means there is no end to sex; it can always become
deeper and more fulfilling.

The more she surrenders, the more energized you become in
your masculine qualities. There is no recipe to open a woman because your efforts must be genuine. Everything that is fake, or
does not come from a deep place within you, will lead to the clo-
sure of her heart. Making love can be heaven on earth, but it de-
pends how deep you are willing to go to understand her thoughts
and feelings.

ONLY THE
DEPTH COUNTS

It's not about how many women you have slept with; it is about how deeply your heart was open and the depth you brought into the bedroom.

When you shift your mindset away from how many women you have slept with, or your achievements in the bedroom, you bring depth and a vulnerable heart into the bedroom.

A masculine man always seeks to experience moments of deep quality, as well as deep presence; thus, you should avoid mindless sex. Mindless sex does not only hurt a woman, but it weakens your presence as a man and creates armor around your heart. It becomes like armor as you misuse the one thing that had the potential to truly open you deeply and make you vulnerable. Instead of telling your buddies how many women you slept with, discuss the depth you brought into the bedroom. Your friends might become irritated hearing you speak like this; however, as an awakened man, your mission and truth are your number one priority. You are willing to risk losing the people who you once referred to as your brothers to live and speak your truth. Share how open your heart was, how deep your breath was, and how vulnerable and freeing the experience was. Share how she surrendered fully and how you witnessed all her beauty.

Each time you are about to engage in mindless sex, ask yourself, "How does this serve the universe?" It probably does not and instead will only serve to hurt you and your partner.

FUCK THE FANCY TECHNIQUES

Make love to her like it is your last day on earth. Kiss her as you would kiss the universe. Touch her as you would touch a tender flower. Lick her into heaven.

The porn paradigm has ruined the sanctity of intimacy. Mechanical body movements, while being stuck in your head, are what some people call "making love." However, when you breathe deeply into your lower stomach and touch her body, she will feel loving shivers of ecstasy in her heart.

When you lick her, imagine drinking from the fountain of light and grace. Her nectar rejuvenates your soul. Set the intention to lick her into heaven, to give her both a bodily and an energetic orgasm, and when you do this, she will form a deep emotional connection with you because you listened to her needs and desires.

Ravish each part of her body. Do not just go all in on her butt, vagina, and breasts. Other parts of her body yearn for your tongue, your presence, and your freedom. It is not about fancy techniques. Fuck the techniques. Rip your heart open and make love to her like it was the last day on earth. This begins with knowing yourself and knowing her, by being in touch with your own mission and listening deeply to her subtle communication.

When your bodies are pressed against each other, and your two tongues touch, you feel united with love and with the divine. Feel it so deeply that your chest breaks open and your consciousness expands. You were born to be a conscious bedroom warrior.

KISSING A WOMAN

When you kiss a woman, feel her soft lips pressed against your heart. You kiss the universe in motion, and she becomes a tender flower, as well as the fresh breeze of a soothing night. Allow her lips and tongue to make love to your soul and ignite the wildest passion.

Kissing a woman can be a means to an end, or it can be a sacred tangle of two lips and two hearts. How deeply present can you be as your lips and tongues meet each other? Can you feel into your body and become aware of her softness and feminine grace washing over you? While you kiss her, be as present as you can. Feel her soft lips, taste her sensual tongue, and listen to her sweet moaning. When the kissing becomes very intense, protect her by holding her hips, with one hand on her lower back. Allow her to forget who she is and to melt in the gentleness and fire of your lips.

BEFORE YOU
ENTER HER

*Ancient tantra describes men as fire and women as water.
Men are most often able to immediately have intercourse;
they don't need much preparation. When it stands, it
stands. Women need time to warm up. She needs to
feel safe in the bedroom; it is your responsibility as the
awakened man to open her fully and allow her juices to
flow like an unstoppable river.*

Before you enter her, make sure her juices are fully flowing.
Make sure she is able to surrender and relax. Only when she
is fully open should you move on to intercourse. Imagine her vulva is like a divine flower, and you are the sun that opens her. If the
flower is not open, its nectar remains hidden. Every time you have
sex with a woman and her juices are not fully flowing, you engage
in an entirely superficial act.

Sacred intimacy is about union with the universe. You cannot
experience raw union without the opening of a woman. Only
when she surrenders are you both able to move deeper into the
essence of the universe and to taste the sweet nectar of passion.

When you lick her, feel the ocean on your tongue, and feel her divine nectar. Let her liquids and juices fill you with passion and ecstasy. When you enter her, enter as softly as you can and be present in the moment. Make sure she feels protected and safe, and hold her gently. When you kiss her, meet her where she is. Kiss her fiercely to demonstrate that she is fierce. Kiss her softly and gently to demonstrate that she is soft and gentle.

Devote yourself fully to the act of union. Do not rush or focus on coming. Focus on this very moment. Sacred intimacy is only as sacred as you make it.

WHEN YOU ARE INSIDE HER

The moment you are inside a woman, you have an immense responsibility. You are not only inside her vulva but her heart, her soul, and her body as well. You do not enter a sacred temple with a cluttered mind. You do not dump your shit on the altar; you honor it, love it, and respect it.

When you are fully present and inside a woman, offer your full masculine heart, remain aware of your deep breath, and support her feminine heart so that she surrenders and feels comfortable with you. Her surrender permits you to drop into the deep embers of your masculine fire. You begin to meet your own strength in motion, and she becomes an embodiment of the sacred structure and direction with which you penetrate the world.

This is the ultimate dance. She becomes dripping wet, and her divine liquids flow like a roaring waterfall. You become a safe, strong mountain with roots that dig deep into the earth, as you are touched by her nectar and feminine expression.

LICKING A WOMAN

While you lick a woman, make sure your breath is deep,
and hold her gently, as the protector of the sacred space.
Massage her breasts and entire body. Licking a woman is
a sacred process that softens your heart and makes you
deeply vulnerable.

Her nectar opens your soul and softens your heart. If you are fully present, you can feel how vulnerable her surrender makes you feel. While you lick her, your hands touch the naked fragility of life. It is so beautiful to experience a woman's naked surrender, and to be the protector and the space-holder, as she experiences one orgasm after the other, safely held in your loving and strong arms.

She wants to let go fully and drop into an ocean of endless love. By creating that space for her, as a conscious leader, you will make her feel safe and turn her on at the deepest level. Lick her into heaven. Make her remember her wild roots. Be the rock in the ocean that protects her naked body from its furious waves.

GIVE HER AN ENERGETIC ORGASM

Many men suffer from performance anxiety. They are afraid of an inability to offer a woman deep pleasure and an orgasm in the bedroom. Do not focus on giving her a physical orgasm; give her an energetic orgasm or one that stems from her happiness and comfort. Allow her to come to your bold authenticity and natural confidence.

When she goes through intense emotions, and you stand your ground and penetrate her with your unwavering love, she experiences an energetic orgasm.

When she starts to speak rudely, collapses, and leans on you and you stand tall like a mountain, rooted into the earth, and meet her with your authentic confidence and relentless commitment to love, she experiences an energetic orgasm because she feels emotionally connected to you.

When she distances herself from you and gives you less attention, and you remain in control of your emotional state and do not become needy or dependent, she experiences an energetic orgasm.

If you are able to penetrate a woman's mood swings, she will trust and surrender fully to you, and your performance anxiety will dissolve into an endless ocean that you will sail courageously upon.

FEMININE
ABUNDANCE

You do not need to make love to a woman in order to receive her feminine heart. When she talks, feel her words echo in your heart. When she moves, feel the reaction in your body. Her elegance and grace open your cells and relieve tension in your muscles. Become a master at receiving a woman's radiance, and you will no longer be a slave to your urges. Get in touch with the abundance of feminine energy that vibrates all around you.

It is very easy to give and serve others, since this is highly rewarded by society, but receiving the fullness of a woman's heart and love is a totally different story. Sometimes men confuse the tender love of a woman with erotic fantasies and connect it to their sexual drive. We tend to eroticize our shadows when we have experienced trauma by being neglected or abused as a child. What this means is that our trauma and intimacy wounds express themselves as obsessive sexual desires. You cannot suppress these desires or meditate them away, but you can do the deep work and get to the root of why you are so obsessed. You can take your intense energetic investment out of them and surrender it to the universe. This is probably one of or even the most difficult challenges for a man to face. It means to go against your own biology and to grow your spiritual muscle in a way that requires all your hunger and determination.

Part of the reason men become addicted to sex is because it is the only way, at least based on their conditioning, to receive the unbound flow of innocent joy and love from a woman. Practice receiving a woman's energy without having sex. Receive her fully, and your sex-life will take on a new level of depth and pleasure.

HEART
CONNECTION

When you are connected to your heart while you make love to a woman, everything starts to change. Her movements become like water, her breath becomes ecstatic, and her vulva swallows you into an endless ocean of love.

Call it God/Universe/Brahman/Atman; you can meet the creator while you make love to a woman. You can taste the creator when you kiss and lick her. A woman's nectar is born from a golden river that rests in the valley of heaven. You can meet the creator's fluidity when you hold space for each of her movements, as her passionate tongue swirls, her radiating vulva swallows your conscious cock, and her tender thighs welcome you into paradise.

Draw as much energy as possible away from your head and back into your body, which is your temple. Feel the strength of your cock in her vulva, feel her naked fragility pressed against your heart, and breathe in her unbelievable tenderness. The more you remain fully conscious and aware of your partner's needs

during sex, the more you will meet the creator, or whatever great-
er force you believe in. It will become an embodied and enlight-
ening experience. Sacred sex will deepen you in a way that meditation rarely does. It is pure devotion, the deepest ecstasy, which
is available here right now, at your fingertips.

CONSCIOUS DOMINANCE

There is nothing wrong with being dominant in the bedroom if you are sensitive to her heart and stay present. Sacred sex is not supposed to be neutral and equal in the sense of "I dominate you 50%, and you dominate me 50%." That's boring. Energetical imbalance in the bedroom is actually a sign of strong erotic friction.

The reason why there is so much heat and tension around the topic of being dominant in the bedroom, as a man, is because many men have become slaves to their sexual urges and disconnected from their heart. These men might be in a place so dark that all hope is lost; however, you, as an awakened man on your journey, can be as dominant as you want to be, if you remain connected to your heart. You do not need to remember to be connected to your heart; simply feel into your body and bring a sense of tenderness and gentleness to your dominance. You could call it "compassionate dominance."

You might take her like a fierce warrior and make her moaning shatter windows, but you must love her through the process and remain sensitive to her heart and rooted in your body. if you have fears, simply tell a woman that you want to practice conscious dominance and that she should tell you if she feels unsafe at any time or if she no longer feels your presence.

Just because you can choose to be consciously dominant doesn't mean you have to be. Maybe you enjoy being dominated by her as well, which does not mean you are not masculine. This is a common toxic belief that stops many men from experiencing deep pleasure in the bedroom.

It is totally fine to switch roles in the bedroom if it aligns with both of you and your needs. Switching roles does not mean necessarily that you switch energetic poles as well. It is less about your actions and more about your presence and the energy you permit.

So, if you like to be dominated as a man, then bring warriorship into the experience. Surrender fully to her. You do not surrender as the feminine; you surrender as the masculine. Sometimes, the most masculine men desire to be dominated at times because it balances them and helps them to soften and surrender more.

Guard these teachings well, they are here for you to create and experience deep intimacy, not to be treated as dogma and played out as another script.

Part 5

HEALING

THE RISE OF
THE FEMININE

The rise of the feminine does not make you weaker; it strengthens you. Women yearn for you to step up as a sacred leader, to penetrate the world with your strong spine and compassionate heart. Masculine energy involves being in service. When we are in deep service to our mission, women, and the future generation, we heal this planet and gain true freedom.

Conscious female leaders are emerging throughout the globe like never before. The more conscious women there are, the more conscious men will follow. The awakened woman gives birth to the awakened man and sharpens him to protect and lead the world.

The feminine does not push you from your throne; she rips your ego apart and gives you a map to your true inner kingdom. Once you have reclaimed your kingdom, there will be no need to compete or compare yourself with any woman or man. There will be no war between genders; there will be deep unity, since everyone is in service to the divine.

The reason why men compete with women and vice versa is because many have not yet realized what their unique calling and gift to the world is. As the feminine partner, your gift is to soften and open the world, to drench it with your radiating light, and to allow the fierceness and wilderness of your heart to guide you. As the masculine, your gift is to protect, to hold the feminine and the world in your arms, and to serve as the presence-holder of the world, as you create a comfortable space for her, remain attentive to her, and maintain your mission all the while.

PROVIDE THE
SACRED SPACE

You cannot imagine how life-changing it is for a woman when you provide the sacred space for her to embody her fullest feminine essence. Permit her to be wild, chaotic, divine, furious, hectic, soft, passionate and alive, or in short, to act like a woman. The more you hold space for her feminine essence, the deeper the intimacy and attraction. You restore order. You heal the damage our ancestors left. We are here to create a new earth that is safe for women on a physical, emotional, and spiritual level, for all future generations to follow.

Your masculine gift is to guide a woman deeper into her feminine heart. You become the sacred riverbanks of her divine waters. You become the rock in the ocean that protects her naked body on the shore. You become the space-holder and the shaman warrior that creates fertile ground for her to blossom. Providing the sacred space can only work if you know who you are and possess a healthy masculine core. The depth of the space you provide for a woman reveals your spiritual depth as man.

Meditate every single day. Ask yourself "Who am I?" multiple times throughout the day. Travel into the rich landscapes of your most inner and intimate being, and you will create a space so sacred that she cannot help herself but drench you in her most radiant light.

HEALING

The masculine can only go as far as the feminine opens, and the feminine can only open as far as the masculine is present. Each needs the other to heal and awaken.

A woman wants to be as open as love and as radiant as light. A man wants to be present to realize his infinite consciousness. In the end, both want to awaken, to heal, to grow, and to be of service.

You can be the most conscious man on earth; however, not every woman will want to open her heart towards you. You can be the most conscious woman on earth, and not every man will realize your pure radiance. We need one another to make this journey work. We need one another to awaken and heal our planet.

Part 6

EPILOGUE

I could have written a thousand pages more, and still not cover the whole spectrum of masculine/feminine dynamics and all of the teachings about the feminine.

These teachings do not work if you apply them dogmatically and have a "black and white approach" towards them. The work is always about embodiment. When you embody the teaching, and you extrapolate what you learn, then utilize it in a manner that works for you, it transcends the conceptual and becomes a felt experience.

An example I like to give is, when you make love to a woman, and you think about how present you should be, or what an awakened man would do right now, then you have just replaced your old script and conditioning with a new one. I have tried this method, and failed miserably. You should aim to be present without having to consciously will it to life.

Similar to how a woman does not always make sense to your rational mind, these teachings extend deeper than the actual written content. It is far wiser to focus on one or two aspects of these teachings and to integrate them in your life, in lieu of trying to become an embodiment of all that has been written in this book. Be gentle with yourself along the process. Do not make it a goal to become the perfect enlightened man. Perfection does not exist. Remember, the feminine does not want a perfect man, but a man who owns his past, continues to show up, and is willing to transcend all the challenges he encounters. The practice lies in facing everything in your journey with presence, curiosity, and openness.

Another important thing is that I write and teach about the ideal, enlightened state in a partnership. Yes, there are many moments in which you can experience the deepest and most profound sex, but do not forget that life comes with ups and downs. You can only truly enjoy and celebrate the peak experiences if you have experienced less exciting moments. Deep intimacy is not about being in the perfect relationship, or experiencing ecstatic pleasure all the time; it is about being radically honest and transparent.

There will be times where you constantly share an amazing connection and experience deep sex, and there will be moments where you will be tested more. In the latter, you have to first descend into the shadows in order to ascend into your raw and authentic power.

The reason why I see intimate relationships as one of the most important elements in life is because deep and healthy intimacy will nourish you like nothing else. Humans are social beings. We are wired to look for a partner, or someone we can experience the highs and lows with. We desire someone that loves and accepts us no matter what.

You can be highly successful and enlightened, but if you have no one to share your experience with, no one to hold you in your pain, and no one to experience physical union with, then you will feel lonely. Now this does not mean that there is anything wrong with being single. Remain single until you find someone with whom you can truly grow, but do not neglect the basic human need to share intimacy, in all its beautiful ways, with one another.

Do not use these teachings to manipulate or strengthen your ego. It can be very tempting, especially when you have already started to embody some of them, to use them in order to gain approval, feel better about yourself, and prove to others how amazing you are. That is not the goal. The idea behind these teachings is to utilize them in a pure, innocent, and heart-centered way. The reason why I do not refer to myself as a dating coach is because I see so many superficial recipes out there that prove highly manipulative and inauthentic. You are here for the real battle, which is the battle of consciousness, in which you must become present in your life in order to truly find happiness in your relationship.

Pick-up artists, fuckboys, or whatever name you want to use, are highly insecure people and will never have access to the kind of intimacy I discuss. I used to possess that energy, and I have never felt more depleted and empty than during that period of my life. The most conscious, most awakened man does not need to show off his skills or prove his greatness to others. He follows his purpose silently and with immense dedication. His results speak volumes and his presence and energy ignite the world.

If you have read this book until the end, then you are part of a great awakening, a new rising of ancient consciousness that will inhabit the lungs of the earth. If you only understand 1% of what has been written, then you are already deep on the path, and I want to honor you for opening your heart and soul.

ABOUT THE AUTHOR

Lorin Krenn is a Deep Intimacy Coach and Writer. His approach to intimate relationships and sex is provocative, radical, and life-altering. He helps men and women all around the globe to experience deep intimacy in their relationships through his podcast, social media appearances, coaching, and workshops.

If you want to learn more about Lorin's work, visit: lorinkrenn.com.

Made in the USA
Coppell, TX
16 March 2021

51807168R10068